This Book Belongs to:

_____

# Authentic

[aw-then-tik]

*(To be real, genuine, and original)*

**Psalm 139:13 (NIV) "For you created my inmost being; you knit me together in my mother's womb."**

Did you know that God made you an original? You are one of a kind, no one like you! The Bible says that He knows you by name and that you have purpose. God has a plan for your life that was written out just for you and by being authentic (genuine, real, and original) you can live out that plan. Just be you!

Every part of you, God knit together. That means He spent time creating you and making you truly special. Have you ever seen someone knit? It's a very involved and time-consuming process and that's how God chose to describe how He made you! God made you authentic for a reason and you should be proud of who you are in Him. At school, with your friends, or even at church it may be hard to appreciate being original and you might want to fit in, but you, awesome daughter of God, were designed to stand out!

## ❣.Prayer.❣

Lord, thank You for creating me and making me authentic. Help me to remember that I am an original and that I am special. Let me live out the real plan You have for my life. In Jesus' name, amen.

# .❣Notes❣.

# Brave

[breyv]

*(Courage to do right and have faith)*

**Deuteronomy 31:6 (Message) "Be strong. Take courage. Don't be intimidated. Don't give them a second thought because God, your God, is striding ahead of you. He's right there with you. He won't let you down; he won't leave you."**

God tells us many times in the Bible to be brave and have faith. When we are afraid, Jesus tells us to cling to Him and He will cover us and keep us safe. You don't have to fear when Jesus is near because He will never leave you alone, so you can be brave because He is with you.

Do you have any fears?

What are they?

Can you give God your fear and be brave?

Sometimes being brave just means being kind when no one else is, to help a friend even when we are not quite sure how, or doing something for Jesus that we would not normally do on our own.

You can be brave in many ways. Trust God and He will show you how to be strong.

## ❥.Prayer.❥

Lord, help me to be braver and show me the areas in my heart that are afraid so that You can make me strong in faith. In Jesus' name, amen.

# .❣Notes❣.

_____
_____
_____
_____
_____
_____
_____
_____
_____
_____
_____
_____
_____
_____
_____
_____
_____
_____
_____
_____
_____
_____
_____
_____

# Confident

[kon-fi-duh nt]

*(Knowing who you are in Christ)*

**Jeremiah 17:7 (NIV) "But blessed is the one who trusts in the LORD, whose confidence is in him."**

God wants you to be confident in Him, which means you must know who you are to Him. God sees you as precious and even when we make mistakes, He still sent His one and only Son, Jesus, to die for us. You can be confident in the fact that Jesus loves you and that He will always be there for you, your family, and friends.

Real self-confidence is Christ-confidence. It's knowing who Jesus really is and depending on His perfection, not on your own.

So who are you in Christ?

You are righteous, victorious, and free. God calls you His friend. Yep, that's right, God calls you His friend, so don't let anyone who is not your friend make you feel bad about yourself. Confidence does not come with outward things, but starts in your heart! Your confidence should always be found in Christ and in Him alone.

## ❥.Prayer.❥

Lord, help me build my confidence in You and let me always hold my head up high and remember I am the daughter of the King! In Jesus' name, amen.

# .❣Notes❣.

# ❣.Dreamer.❣

[dree-mer]

(Dreaming Godly dreams)

**Philippians 4:13 (NIV) "I can do all this through him who gives me strength."**

Whatever your dreams are, whether you want to be a singer, athlete, teacher, musician, writer, scientist, etc., place your dreams in God's hands because when you give God your dreams He can make them come true.

And dreams are not always like a Disney fairy tale. Most of the time you have to work very hard toward your goals and dreams to make them a reality, but with God, you can do it. He will give you the wisdom and favor to do what you set your heart out to do.

God knows the desires of your heart and He wants to bless you. You just have to do your part and do what you can, and He can do the impossible. God can open up doors for your dreams, and will, as long as you choose to honor Him in all that you do. I believe you can do anything you work hard at and put your mind to, so keep studying, practicing, and reaching high!

## ❤.Prayer.❤

Lord, I pray my dreams are godly and honor You. Help me to work hard towards what I want for my life and help me accomplish my dreams. In Jesus' name, amen.

# .⋅❣Notes❣⋅.

_____

_____

_____

_____

_____

_____

_____

_____

_____

_____

_____

_____

_____

_____

_____

_____

_____

_____

_____

_____

_____

_____

_____

_____

# .:Encourager♥

[en-kur-i-jer]

(To encourage others)

**1 Thessalonians 5:11 (NIV) "Therefore encourage one another and build each other up, just as in fact you are doing."**

Did you know that God wants you to lift others up with your words, actions, and attitude? You can encourage your friends, teachers, mom and dad, and even your brothers and sisters!

How?

You can encourage others by being the light of Jesus Christ. Let others know that they are doing good. If you really like something someone did, let them know! That will encourage them and probably even put a smile on their face. Work on saying only uplifting things and work really hard on not saying mean, hurtful things. Think about what you say and do, and ask yourself if you are being the encourager God wants you to be. Even a good attitude will encourage others when they are around you. By being an encourager you can change someone's entire day!

# ♥.Prayer.♥

Lord, let me think before I speak and help me to uplift and encourage others when they are down. Let me be the encourager someone else needs. In Jesus' name, amen.

# Notes

# Forgiving

[for-giv-ing]

*(To forgive others)*

**Mark 11:25 (NLT) "But when you are praying, first forgive anyone you are holding a grudge against, so that your Father in heaven will forgive your sins, too."**

Do you hold grudges? You know the type of thing where someone may hurt you, so you stay mad at them because of what they had done to you. Did you know the Bible teaches us to not hold grudges against others?

God wants us to forgive even when it's hard. He wants us to forgive that friend who may have hurt our feelings and forgive our brother who annoys us and forgive those who have wronged us.

Forgiving is even hard for adults to do and will be something that you learn to do with each time you do it. The more you forgive, the more God can heal you of the hurt others have caused. I know sometimes people can be really mean, but you know God forgave you, so you can forgive them. When you are upset or mad at someone, take a deep breath, and forgive. Don't hold on to any grudges because grudges will hurt your heart. Forgiving will help heal your heart.

Lord, help me to forgive and move forward in life when other people have done wrong against me. I let go of my grudges and give You my pain. Thank You for being my healer from the hurt others have caused. In Jesus' name, amen.

# Notes

# Generous

[jen-er-uh s]

*(To give to others)*

**1 Timothy 6:18 (NIV) "Command them to do good, to be rich in good deeds, and to be generous and willing to share."**

Jesus wants those who love Him and follow Him to be as generous as He is, and He is very generous. We should be ready to do good works and be willing to share with others that which we have to help them.

Sometimes others go through really hard times and it would be a real blessing for you to lend a hand. When we follow Christ, we are blessed so that we can turn around and bless others.

You can be generous with your time and volunteer

at an animal shelter, food bank, or hospital. You could even visit the elderly at a retirement home and read to them.

There are a lot of ways to be generous and give back. Talk to your parents, grandparents, or guardian to see how you can be generous in your community.

## ❣Prayer❣

Lord, help me to live generously and give back where I can. Let me be willing to share and quick to do good unto others. Show me somehow I can be more giving of my time, gifts, and talents. In Jesus' name, amen.

# .⁙Notes⁙.

_____
_____
_____
_____
_____
_____
_____
_____
_____
_____
_____
_____
_____
_____
_____
_____
_____
_____
_____
_____
_____
_____
_____
_____

# .꙳Honest.꙳

[on-ist]

(To tell the truth)

**Proverbs 12:17 (NIV) "An honest witness tells the truth, but a false witness tells lies."**

God wants us to be very honest, even when it's hard to tell the truth. Telling the truth honors God and brings reward, but telling a lie will get you in trouble and could even cause harm.

Be honest with yourself, parents, and teachers. Have an honest answer when a question is asked and work really hard on just telling the truth. There's an old saying that says, "Honesty is the best policy." And it's true, honesty is the best way to go, even when you are in trouble and you think lying would be better, or would keep you out of trouble.

Yes, telling the truth may be hard, but telling a lie is even harder because then others will not know if they can trust you. Be as honest as you would want someone to be with you. You probably don't like to be lied to; neither do others, so no more lies. Tell the truth with kindness and love.

Lord, help me to be honest with others and to tell the truth. Work on my heart and the reasons why I lie so that I can be free to be honest. In Jesus' name, amen.

# ❤:Notes:❤

# Inspired

[in-spahyuh rd]

*(To be creative in Christ)*

**Ephesians 2:10 (ESV) "...created in Christ Jesus for good works..."**

God gave each one of us a special gift and He wants us to be inspired and give that gift back to Him. God will often give you an idea in your heart that uses what you're good at. Be inspired and run with it!

Let God spark creative ideas in you and use the talent He has given you to create something beautiful. You can write a song, choreograph a dance, draw a piece of art, speak to others, or start your very own club.

You can be so inspired that you can inspire others and then they can be creative and make something beautiful too!

What inspires you?

Think of some ways where you can use your gifts and talents to glorify God and inspire others. You were meant to be inspired and be creative for Christ! Have fun and serve the Lord with the ideas He gives you. You have talent! Use it!

## ⁖Prayer⁖

Lord, I pray that every talent You have given me I give back to You. Help me to be motivated and inspired to do creative things for You! In Jesus' name, amen.

# .⁚Notes⁚.

# ❣Joyful❣

[joi-fuh l]

*(To be happy)*

**Psalms 68:3 (NIV) "But may the righteous be glad and rejoice before God; may they be happy and joyful."**

God wants you to be happy; there is no doubt about that. But sometimes there will be times when you are not happy, so what do you do? When you are not happy, or when something does not go your way, remember where your happiness is found.

God wants us to be happy in Him. Happy to know Him. Happy to follow Him. Happy to be His daughter. Happiness is not always about getting things, going on a trip, or everything working out just like you want it. Real happiness comes from

God and only He can make you truly joyful (joy-filled).

When you are not happy, instead of thinking about all of the bad, think about all of the good God has done for you. God has done a lot for you to be happy about, so think about that, smile, and let God be the One to make you happy because His joy never fails and makes us strong!

## ❥.Prayer.❥

Lord, let me find my happiness in You and Your Word. When things go wrong, help me to keep my joy because I know the joy of the Lord is my strength. In Jesus' name, amen.

# .❣Notes❣.

# Kind

[kahynd]

*(To be nice to others)*

**Ephesians 4:32 (NIV) "Be kind and compassionate to one another..."**

Being kind to others is one of the most Christ-like things you can do. Think about a time when someone was nice to you. Now, think about how that made you feel.

Didn't it feel good to have someone be kind to you?

Think about how all of your kindness can make others feel. Don't you want them to feel how you felt when someone was nice to you?

Be kind to others and treat them as you wish to be treated. Your kindness to others could quite possibly change the world!

Don't be afraid to be kind. Think about all the ways that you might be able to show kindness to your friends, parents, grandparents, and siblings.

Do you have any ideas?

What is one way you can be kind today?

## ❥.Prayer.❥

Lord, let me be kind to others and show them compassion. Show me ways that I can be kind everywhere I go. In Jesus' name, amen.

# .꙰Notes꙰.

# Loving

[luhv-ing]

*(To love like Jesus)*

**John 13:34 (NIV) "A new command I give you: Love one another. As I have loved you, so you must love one another."**

What does it really mean to love like Christ, anyway?

Have you ever asked that question?

To love like Christ means to love with all of your heart, forgive, be kind, be compassionate, and willing to serve others.

Sound familiar?

We covered some of those already. So what does loving others mean to you? How can *you* love like

Christ? Jesus taught us how to love in the Bible. He told us to love everyone, no matter what they look like, or where they're from. Jesus loved selflessly, which means He put others first and thought about their needs, hurts, and feelings.

To love like Christ means to care for others like He did and I know we can do that with His help!

## ❤.Prayer.❤

Lord, help me to love like You love. Let me love my neighbor and brothers and sisters like You want me to love them. Help me to have selfless love like You! In Jesus' name, amen.

# .꙳Notes꙳.

# .❤/\odest.❤

[mod-ist]

*(To honor God in behavior and dress)*

**1 Timothy 2:9 (NET) "Likewise the women are to dress in suitable apparel, with modesty and self-control."**

God likes everything to be done nicely and in order. Craziness and wild living does not please God. God asks us to live and dress modestly to allow our true beauty to shine through, which comes from the heart.

When you get dressed for the day, ask God, "Lord, does this honor You?"

It's good to start this practice young so that when you're older you are already in the habit of modesty. God also wants us to behave modestly, which means He does not want us to throw tantrums or fits, or use ugly ungodly words.

To live modestly means to honor God in all that we do, including the way we walk, talk, and behave.

What is modesty to you?

Do you think it will be hard to be modest?

What can you do to be modest?

# ❣.Prayer.❣

Lord, help me to be modest in all that I do so that I may please You and honor You with my whole life. In Jesus' name, amen.

# .⁚Notes⁚.

# Noble

[noh-buh l]

(Moral excellence & of good character)

**Psalm 16:3 (NIV) "I say of the holy people who are in the land, "They are the noble ones in whom is all my delight.""**

Did you know that it makes God happy when you do noble (right) things? God is pleased when you have good moral character and live like He has asked.

Sometimes doing right and being noble is not easy and sets you apart from your friends, but keep doing right! When you do right, God will reward you, for He rewards obedience.

Even if it's super hard, do what you know is right

and you will be blessed for it. God is looking for those who are living right and keeping His commands.

What are some of God's commands you can follow to be noble?

How can you keep good character?

# ❖.Prayer.❖

Lord, help me to be noble and live according to Your Word. Let me be brave enough to do the right thing even when others are doing the wrong thing. In Jesus' name, amen.

# .❤Notes❤.

# Overcomer

[oh-ver-kuhm-er]

*(To overcome the bad in life)*

**Romans 12:21 (NIV) "Do not be overcome by evil, but overcome evil with good."**

Sometimes in life bad things happen, even to good people, and it's hard to know how to overcome them, but God has given us a way through Jesus Christ to overcome.

God says that we overcome by the Blood of the Lamb and the word of our testimony. We can overcome because Jesus has already overcome this world.

All the evil, hate, and hurt...Jesus can heal. He's got you! Give your worries and troubles to Him and He will help you overcome.

Jesus is greater in us than any evil in the world. Next time you feel down and like you are losing, remember, Jesus will help you overcome! He is fighting for you to win and praying for your faith! You can overcome!

## ❥.Prayer.❥

Lord, help me to overcome what I am afraid of and all the hurt that I feel. I pray that I overcome evil, hate, and ugliness with goodness, love, and hope. In Jesus' name, amen.

# .:❤Notes❤:.

# Peaceful

[pees-fuh l]

*(To live at peace)*

**2 Thessalonians 3:16 (NIV) "Now may the Lord of peace himself give you peace at all times and in every way."**

God wants you to have peace. He does not want you to be anxious or always worrying. He wants you to know that He is in control and that you can cast all your cares on Him, no matter what they are.

All of your worries, troubles, and fears, God can take care of them. He is bigger than them all!

Trust God, and know that there is no need to fear or worry. God can give you peace that no one else can, even in the middle of a storm. So, no matter what you are going through, lean on God, and let Him give you peace over your troubles.

Not only does God want you to be at peace, but He wants you to live at peace with others as well. When a fight breaks out between your friends and they all stop talking, be the one that brings peace.

Lord, I pray for peace over my troubles. Help me to give you everything that worries or troubles me so that You can trade it for Your peace that passes all understanding. In Jesus' name, amen.

# .♥.Notes♥.

# Quiet

[kwahy-it]

*(To listen more than you speak)*

**1 Peter 3:3-4 (NIV) "Your beauty should not come from outward adornment, such as elaborate hairstyles and the wearing of gold jewelry or fine clothes. Rather, it should be that of your inner self, the unfading beauty of a gentle and quiet spirit, which is of great worth in God's sight."**

Did you know that sometimes it's okay to be quiet...To just sit still and listen?

Being loud is okay sometimes too, but God speaks to us when we settle down and listen. God often comes as a still, small voice and we have to be ready to listen, which means we have to be quiet.

When do you have quiet time?

Have you ever thought about using that time to pray and listen for the Lord?

When you read your Bible, take a moment to listen too. God speaks to those who are willing to be quiet and listen.

## ❣.Prayer.❣

Lord, I pray that I am quiet enough to hear Your voice and that the world's loudness does not make me lose my focus. In Jesus' name, amen.

# .:Notes:.

# Ready

[red-ee]

*(Ready to be used of God and do good)*

**Titus 3:1 (NIV) "Remind the people to be subject to rulers and authorities, to be obedient, to be ready to do whatever is good."**

Jesus wants everyone who follows Him to be ready to do good, ready to talk about Him to others, and ready for His return. Yes, Jesus is coming again!

How can you be ready to do all those things?

#1 – Stay in your Word! Read the Bible every single day, even if it is one verse. It's that important!

#2 – Pray! Praying is not hard. All you have to do is talk to God as if He is your friend because, guess what, He is! He wants for you to talk to Him and let Him know even about the small things in your life.

#3 – Follow His instructions! God gives us instructions on how to live to keep us safe and make us ready.

Are you ready for God to use you?

## ❥.Prayer.❥

Lord, help me to be ready to do good and tell others about Your goodness. I pray that I endure and am ready for when You decide to return and until You do, use me! In Jesus' name, amen.

# .:Notes:.

_____
_____
_____
_____
_____
_____
_____
_____
_____
_____
_____
_____
_____
_____
_____
_____
_____
_____
_____
_____
_____
_____

# .∵Selfless.∵

[self-lis]

*(To think of others and deny self)*

**Matthew 16:24 (ESV) "If anyone would come after me, let him deny himself and take up his cross and follow me."**

God wants to increase in our lives so there is more of Him and less of us, meaning He wants us to be like Him.

Jesus is the perfect example of selflessness. If you follow His example, then every day, you will be picking up your cross and following Him, and every day you follow Him, you can become a little more like Him.

Look at everything in your heart, even the secrets that you tell no one else...are any of them selfish?

Could you be more selfless in any area of your life? Could you think of how others feel more?

Selfishness is natural, so we will have to fight hard not to allow what we want to get in the way of what God wants.

## ❖.Prayer.❖

Lord, help me to see the areas in my heart and life where I am selfish and help me to become more selfless like You. In Jesus' name, amen.

# .♥Notes♥.

# Thankful

[thangk-fuh l]

*(To give thanks)*

**1 Thessalonians 5:18 (NIV) "Give thanks in all circumstances; for this is God's will for you in Christ Jesus."**

Being thankful is one of the best things you can do not only for others' sake, but for yours as well. Thankfulness allows your heart to be whole and happy.

Think of some things you are thankful for…

Can you write a thank you note to someone to let them know how thankful you are for all they have done?

The thing about being thankful is that you can't keep it to yourself. It will flow over to others and show in your words and actions.

Show how thankful you are to God every day by waking up and saying 'thank you' to Him. He deserves our thankfulness! He is good!

## ❖.Prayer.❖

Lord, I thank You! Help me to see all the good You have done for me and let me be thankful toward You and others. Show me ways to be thankful and let me be full of thanks at all times. In Jesus' name, amen.

# .:Notes:.

_____

_____

_____

_____

_____

_____

_____

_____

_____

_____

_____

_____

_____

_____

_____

_____

_____

_____

_____

_____

_____

_____

# ::Unique::

[yoo-neek]

*(special, set apart, and extraordinary)*

**1 Peter 2:9 (NIV) "But you are a chosen people, a royal priesthood, a holy nation, God's special possession, that you may declare the praises of him who called you out of darkness into his wonderful light."**

God called you to be different, to be set apart from normal, so it's okay to not be normal! You don't have to be like anyone else, all you have to be is you!

God created each one of us uniquely. Did you know that no two people are exactly the same? Not even identical twins!

Every person on earth is unique, and fearfully and

wonderfully made. God chose you to be YOU and no one else. You are beautiful the way He created you and you don't have to fit in with the crowd. You were called out of darkness and into light, and that makes you pretty unique all on its own.

I believe you are extraordinary and will do great, unique things that only you can do with your life!

# ❣.Prayer.❣

Lord, help me to understand my true worth and beauty. Let me appreciate the fact that I am unique and that there is no one else like me! In Jesus' name, amen.

# .❥Notes❥.

# Victorious

[vik-tawr-ee-uh s]

*(Winning in the Lord)*

**Revelation 21:7 (NIV) "Those who are victorious will inherit all this, and I will be their God and they will be my children."**

Have you ever won a sports game or a board game or class game? It's fun to win, right?

What if I told you that Jesus wants you to win?

Well, that's exactly what He wants. Jesus wants you to win at life and eternity. He wants you to gain victory through Him because the only way we win in the end is if we go through Him.

Jesus brings victory through the cross and He has already fought the battle and won the war. We win because He has already won!

To know Jesus and have Him in our hearts means we are victorious.

God is our victory and we are His victorious children.

You win!

## ❥.Prayer.❥

Lord, remind me that I have the victory because of You! Help me to remember that I win in the end because of all that You have done for me! In Jesus' name, amen.

# .:Notes:.

**[wahyz]**

*(To be smart in the Lord)*

**Ecclesiastes 9:16 (NIV) "Wisdom is better than strength."**

God wants us to know about Him and be smart with our lives and the way we live. He will give us wisdom if we ask for it.

In the Bible, a man named Solomon asked God for wisdom over everything else and God gave it to him, and he was able to rule an entire kingdom fairly because of the wisdom God gave.

You can surely live well when you ask God to give you wisdom. He will help you navigate life and everything that happens to you. He can help hold your world together and teach you how to respond in wisdom to situations that are out of your control.

Wisdom can also help you in your future when you have to make tough choices.

Would you like God to give you wisdom as He did Solomon?

All you have to do is ask for it!

# ❣.Prayer.❣

Lord, help me to be wise in all that I do. Order my steps and direct my path. I pray that I always use your wisdom over my understanding. In Jesus' name, amen.

# .:Notes:.

(excited about Jesus♥)

**Psalm 150: 1-6 (ESV) "Praise the Lord! Praise God in his sanctuary; praise him in his mighty heavens! Praise him for his mighty deeds; praise him according to his excellent greatness! Praise him with trumpet sound; praise him with lute and harp! Praise him with tambourine and dance; praise him with strings and pipe! Praise him with sounding cymbals; praise him with loud clashing cymbals!"**

That scripture has a lot of excitement in it, doesn't it? David wrote a lot of Psalms in the Bible and is known as a man after God's own heart, and I believe part of that was because of how excited he was for the things of God.

When you are a girl after God's own heart, you will be excited and want to praise Him like this Psalm says. Get excited about Jesus! Praise Him and just like you would when you're excited with your friends, jump and clap for Jesus when you are excited about Him because He is mighty!

## ❧.Prayer.❧

Lord, let me be excited about You and Your Kingdom! I pray that I praise You and am excited about who You are to me all the days of my life. In Jesus' name, amen.

# .ᴥNotesᴥ.

_____
_____
_____
_____
_____
_____
_____
_____
_____
_____
_____
_____
_____
_____
_____
_____
_____
_____
_____
_____
_____
_____
_____

# .:Youthful:.

[yooth-fuh l]

(It's okay to be young and serve God♥)

**1 Timothy 4:12 (NIV) "Don't let anyone look down on you because you are young, but set an example for the believers in speech, in conduct, in love, in faith and in purity."**

It's okay if you're small, and it's okay if you're young! God can use you!

Sometimes, when you are young, you think that God can't use you and that you have to wait until you are older, but that's not true. God can use you right now, no matter how young you are.

Sometimes God will use you to show your parents His love. Sometimes He will use you to show your teachers His grace. Just because you are young does not mean that you are not mighty!

God can use anyone at any age for His purpose and that means He can use you!

Being young is a gift. God even told us to have child-like faith! Give God your life when you are young and He will bless you greatly when you are older! And, remember, you are not too young!

Jesus can use anyone!

## ❤.Prayer.❤

Lord, remind me every day that even though I may be young that You can still use me greatly. I pray that my life is always Yours and that I never stray from the path You have for my life. In Jesus' name, amen.

# .:Notes:.

_____
_____
_____
_____
_____
_____
_____
_____
_____
_____
_____
_____
_____
_____
_____
_____
_____
_____
_____
_____
_____

# Zealous

[zel-uh s]

*(To have active, eager faith)*

**Proverbs 23:17 (NIV) "...always be zealous..."**

Zealous is a fun word! It means to be enthusiastic, eager, and active. As we come to a close on who God wants us to be from A to Z, let God work in your faith.

Believe that He can use you, work in you, and help you throughout all of your life.

God is a good God and to be zealous for Him means to have active faith and to be eager to serve Him. Your life was made for more than the ordinary.

You are a mighty girl of God and can do whatever He has called you to do because He will help you and see you through it.

I believe in you! You are awesome and have a call of God on your life. Don't be afraid to be different and don't be afraid to love God in a big way!

## ❥.Prayer.❥

Lord, I love You. I want to live for You and serve You with zeal all the days of my life. Let me always seek You and I pray my heart is Yours forever. I am Yours and You are mine. In Jesus' name, amen.

# .:Notes:.

# Questions

♥What is your favorite Bible verse? Why?

♥What Bible verse would you like to memorize that you haven't yet? Write it down!

♥Which story in the Bible is your favorite? Why?

♥Can you think of one thing that you could work on to be more like Jesus? What is it?

♥How can you shine the light of Jesus?

♥Could you be more helpful at home? How?

♥Is there a friend you can encourage?

♥Can you think of anything you need help with? Try to find a Bible verse to help you!

♥Have you given everything you are afraid of to Jesus? He can help you with your fears!

♥What is your biggest dream?

# .:Notes:.

# .:Notes:.

# .:Notes:.

# .:Notes:.

# Notes

# Doodle

## Pages ♥

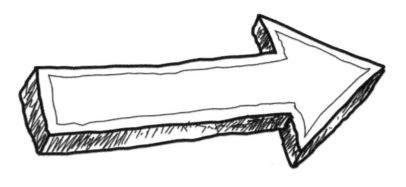

beYOUtiful

# God is

## Love

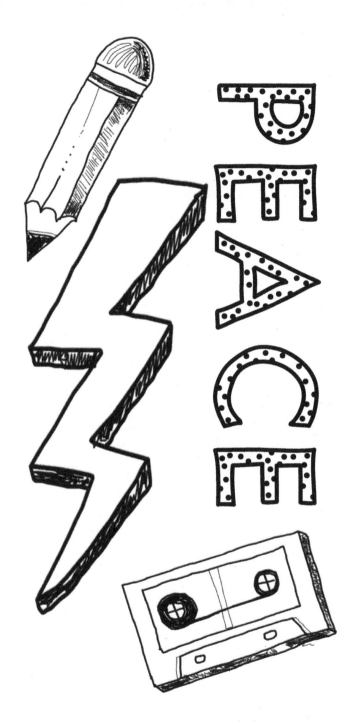

# YOU'RE

# AWESOME!

# Pray!

# FOLLOW JESUS

# DREAM

*idea*

# BIG

have

COURAGE

# Psalm 91:4

He will cover you with his feathers, and under his wings you will find refuge

Trust

Jesus

# THANK YOU for READING!

## .:Mighty God Girl CLUB.:

Welcome to the Mighty God Girl Club, mighty girl!

Remember to pray and read your Bible every single day to stay strong in the Lord!

You are loved, Mighty God Girl!

You are beautiful, Mighty God Girl!

God has a plan for you, Mighty God Girl!

Keep dreaming big, Mighty God Girl!

Rise up, Mighty God Girl, there is work to do for Jesus and you are just the one to do it!

♥

Dear Parents & Guardians,

First, I want to say THANK YOU for getting this book! If you and your Mighty God Girl enjoyed the devotionals, I would love if you would consider leaving a review on Amazon to help spread the word to other Mighty God Girls!

Blessings,

Mandy Fender

**Feel free to connect with me online, I love to hear from readers!**

Twitter: @mandyfender11

Facebook: Mandy Fender

Instagram: Mandy.Fender